100%

← GET THE WHOLE PICTURE →

SPACE AND TIME

PAUL MASON

Cavendish
Square

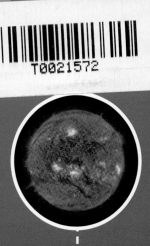

Published in 2024 by Cavendish Square Publishing, LLC
2544 Clinton Street, Buffalo, NY 14224

First published in Great Britain in 2020 by Wayland
Copyright © Hodder and Stoughton, 2020

Website: cavendishsq.com

This publication represents the opinions and views of the author based on his or her personal experience, knowledge, and research. The information in this book serves as a general guide only. The author and publisher have used their best efforts in preparing this book and disclaim liability rising directly or indirectly from the use and application of this book.

All websites were available and accurate when this book was sent to press.

Series editor: Elise Short
Produced by Tall Tree Ltd
Editor: Lara Murphy
Designer: Jonathan Vipond

Picture Credits
t-top, b-bottom, l-left, r-right, c-center, front cover-fc, back cover-bc
bc tr NASA and the Hubble Heritage Team, 1tl and 11t shutterstock/shaineast, tr and 21ct shutterstock/Dotted Yeti, bl and 18 bl shutterstock/yulia_lavrova, br, 20l, 22–23 shutterstock/Triff, 2 and 6 shutterstock/shooarts, 3cr, 27c shutterstock/Designua, 4–5 shutterstock/Triff, 5tr shutterstock/ Triff, 7cr shutterstock/fizyk5, 8tr shutterstock/Elena Korn, b shutterstock/MysticaLink, 9c shutterstock/ capitanoproductions, cr shutterstock/Dima Zel, 10l shutterstock/MarcelClemens, 10–11 shutterstock/ NASA images, 12–13 NASA / WMAP Science Team, 14tr shutterstock/tuntekron petsajun, cl shutterstock/Fred Fokkelman, c shutterstock/Mopic, bl shutterstock/Prosto Vov4ik, bcl shutterstock/ zapolzun, bcr and br shutterstock/artifex.orlova, 15tl shutterstock/Alex Mit, bl, cr, br shutterstock/ Marusya Chaika, 16 shutterstock/Lonely, 17tl shutterstock/VectorShow, tr shutterstock/Pixel Embargo, br shutterstock/NASA images, 18–19 shutterstock/NASA images, 19 tr NASA, 19b shutterstock/NASA images, 20 cl, c, r shutterstock/NASA images, 20 cr shutterstock/robert_s, 20–21c shutterstock/NASA images, 21tl, cl, c, cr shutterstock/NASA images, 23tr shutterstock/maradon 333, 23b all shutterstock/ Marusya Chaika, 24–25t shutterstock/Anton Shahrai, 24–25b shutterstock/leeborn, 26–27 shutterstock/matrioshka, 26bl shutterstock/alice-photo, 28tl shutterstock/Eddie J. Rodriquez, 28bl shutterstock/Looper, 28–29 shutterstock/brichaus, 29tr shutterstock/mkos83

Cataloging-in-Publication Data

Names: Mason, Paul.
Title: Space and time / Paul Mason.
Description: Buffalo, New York : Cavendish Square Publishing, 2024. | Series: 100% get the whole picture | Includes glossary and index.
Identifiers: ISBN 9781502668783 (pbk.) | ISBN 9781502668790 (library bound) | ISBN 9781502668806 (ebook)
Subjects: LCSH: Solar system--Juvenile literature. | Cosmology--Juvenile literature. | Time--Juvenile literature.
Classification: LCC QB501.3 M376 2024 | DDC 523.2--dc23

CPSIA compliance information: Batch #CSCSQ24: For further information contact Cavendish Square Publishing LLC at 1-877-980-4450.

Printed in the United States of America

Find us on

CONTENTS

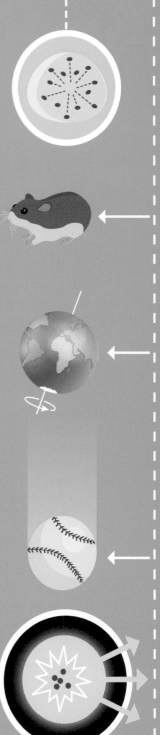

Space and time 4

The Big Bang.........................6

Space 8

The universe 10

Dark matter.........................12

Stars 14

Black holes 16

Galaxies..............................18

The solar system 20

The sun 22

Earth 24

Hours and days 26

Standardizing time 28

Glossary and
further information.................. 30

Index 32

All measurements in this book are presented in metric, as they are the units most scientists prefer to work in.

Space and time

When people talk about "space" or "outer space," they mean the stars, planets, and other celestial bodies, like asteroids. Plus all the … well, space between them—and everything in it.

Big thinking

Space and everything in it is known as universe. The universe is made up of hundreds of billions of galaxies.

Galaxies are made up of billions of stars.

Circling around the stars are planets and other objects.

SCIENTISTS ESTIMATE THAT THE NUMBER OF STARS IN THE UNIVERSE IS ABOUT 70 SEXTILLION (A SEXTILLION IS A 1 FOLLOWED BY 21 ZEROS), BUT NO ONE REALLY KNOWS FOR SURE.

38,000,000,000,000 km

DISTANCE TO PROXIMA CENTAURI, THE SECOND-NEAREST STAR TO EARTH.

Our closest star is the sun. Even the sun is so far away (about 149,600,000 km!) that it takes about eight minutes for its light to reach Earth.

The start of space and time

Scientists think that the universe and time both began at the same instant. They call this moment the Big Bang (see pages 6–7).

Because time began at that point, there is no "before" the Big Bang.

The universe exploded into existence in a "Big Bang."

Gravity

One of the most important forces in the universe is gravity, a pulling force.

All matter has gravity: stars, planets, people, hamsters—even the tiniest particles.

Gravity pulls objects together. Big objects have greater gravity than small ones. In space, for example, smaller planets are drawn toward larger stars.

The Big Bang

The Big Bang theory was proposed by astronomer Georges Lemaître in 1927. Scientists believe that the Big Bang took place about 13.74 billion years ago.

Stars started to form after about 200 million years.

Zooming in

A moment after the Big Bang, the universe was contained in a single tiny point—smaller even than an atom.

After the Big Bang, an enormous number of tiny particles, far smaller than atoms, began to spread rapidly outward.

100%
OF THE MATTER IN THE UNIVERSE CAME FROM THE BIG BANG

Exploding universe

The Big Bang was incredibly powerful. Within the first second, the universe was already billions of miles across, and the first particles had formed.

5,500,000,000°C

THE TEMPERATURE IN THE FIRST
SECOND AFTER THE BIG BANG
CREATED THE UNIVERSE

The universe today

Today, the universe is still
getting bigger (see pages
10–11).

- Its galaxies are moving
  ever farther from the
  site of the Big Bang.
- The most distant
  galaxies are
  moving away
  more quickly.

Eventually, some
galaxies will be
moving away from
us faster than the
speed of light.
They will no longer
be visible from Earth.

distant galaxies in outer space

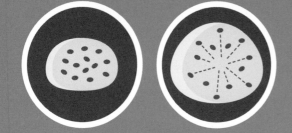

Expanding bread

If you bake a raisin loaf, you'll see the raisins
near the outside of the loaf spread out
faster than those nearer to the center. This
phenomenon models the way galaxies are
speeding away from each other.

299,792,458
meters per second
SPEED AT WHICH LIGHT TRAVELS

Space

Space begins about 100 km above Earth's surface.
Up there, there is no air and the sky is always black.

Mapping space

Astronomers have been peering into space
through telescopes since the time of Italian
Galileo Galilei (1564–1642). The regions of space
close to Earth have been carefully mapped, but
as the distance from Earth increases, we know
less and less about exactly what is out there.

astronomer Galileo Galilei

**Experts
estimate that:**

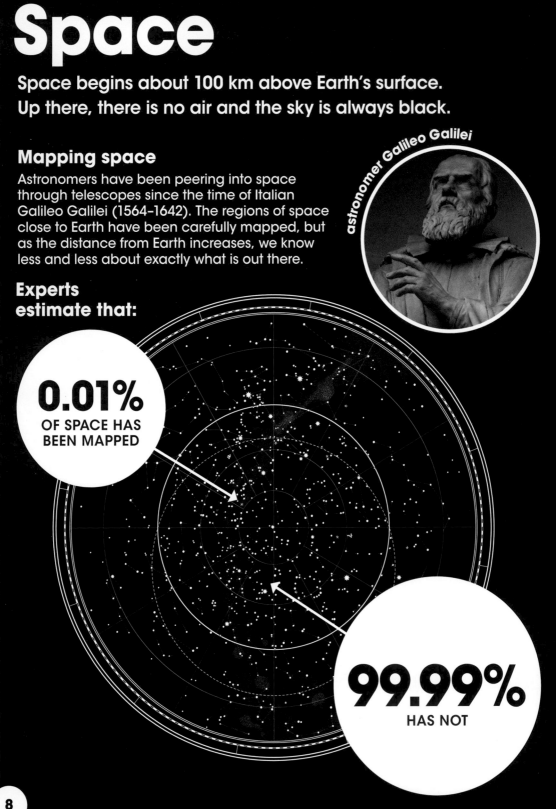

0.01%
OF SPACE HAS
BEEN MAPPED

99.99%
HAS NOT

Silent space ...

Because there is no air in space, there is also no sound. Air is needed for sound to travel from one place to another.*

*Which makes the idea of a Big BANG a bit odd, when you think about it.

... not empty space

Space is silent, but it is not empty.

- Many types of radiation (a form of energy) travel through space. Astronauts have to be protected from radiation from the sun as well as X-rays, gamma rays, and cosmic rays from other stars.

- Space also contains thinly spread clouds of gas, dust, and other particles.

Space junk

The area of space close to Earth is crowded with objects we sometimes call "space junk."

This includes:

- old satellites (artificial objects orbiting Earth)

- abandoned parts of old spacecraft

Space suits protect astronauts from radiation.

Satellite or space junk?

20,000+

ESTIMATED NUMBER OF PIECES OF SPACE JUNK LARGER THAN A SOFTBALL (10 CM ACROSS)

Some space junk is travelling at more than 28,000 kph—six times as fast as the fastest bullet.

As it orbits Earth, the International Space Station (ISS) sometimes has to change position to avoid hitting bits of space junk.

The universe

In 1929, astronomer Edwin Hubble discovered that space is constantly getting bigger. Telescopes in orbit around Earth have shown astronomers that this has been happening ever since the Big Bang.

The Hubble Space Telescope is named after Edwin Hubble.

Matter vs. antimatter

Right after the Big Bang, most energy was either matter or antimatter (particles that are the opposite of matter).

• The two mostly destroyed each other immediately.

• There was more matter than antimatter to start with, so what was left was mostly matter.

The leftover matter formed tiny particles called protons, neutrons, and electrons.

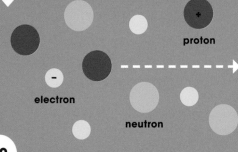

proton

electron

neutron

Cooling universe

Within three minutes, the temperature had dropped from 5,500,000,000°C to less than 1,000,000,000°C.

As the universe cooled, it began to take shape. Protons and neutrons joined together to form nuclei.

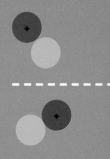

93,000,000,000 light-years

A light-year is the distance light travels in one year— about 9.4 trillion km.

The distances are so massive it would take a fighter jet over 1 million years just to fly to the star system nearest to our sun: Alpha Centauri (about 4 million light-years from Earth).

25%
IS HELIUM

1%
IS HEAVIER ELEMENTS, SUCH AS CARBON AND OXYGEN

74%
OF THE UNIVERSE'S KNOWN MASS IS HYDROGEN

Stars and galaxies

Clouds of hydrogen and helium gas began to fill the universe. Once the temperature cooled, stars and galaxies were born from these clouds.

Hydrogen and helium

After 380,000 years, the universe's temperature had dropped to about 3,000°C. The nuclei began to combine with electrons to form atoms. Most were hydrogen and helium atoms.

helium atom

hydrogen atom

Dark matter

In this cosmic radiation map of the early universe, different colors show different temperatures.

We cannot see dark matter, but scientists think it has to exist. They know more about what it ISN'T than what it is.

Dark evidence

Scientists think dark matter must exist because:

- they measured the amount of radiation left over from the Big Bang
- the matter we know about would not be enough to produce so much radiation

This shows that there must be far more matter in the universe than scientists know about.

Scientists think the universe is made up of:

5%
ATOMIC MATTER
(THE KIND WE UNDERSTAND, MADE OF ATOMS)

27%
DARK MATTER
(THE KIND WE REALLY DON'T UNDERSTAND)

What dark matter is ...

The only thing we know for sure about dark matter (apart from that it must be there) is that it is dark, meaning we cannot see it.

What dark matter isn't ...

Dark matter is not:

- stars, planets, or any other celestial body we know about
- dark clouds of normal matter
- antimatter

What dark matter might be ...

Scientists have two leading ideas:

MACHOS, or Massive Compact Halo Objects, are either black holes (see pages 16–17) or the remains of massive stars.

WIMPS, or Weakly Interacting Massive Particles, are tiny particles that are not ordinary matter. (They are "massive" because they have mass, not because they are huge.)

68%
DARK ENERGY
(A MYSTERY FORM OF ENERGY)

Dark energy

We know dark energy must be there because something is causing the universe to expand faster and faster. Apart from that, dark energy is even more mysterious than dark matter.

Stars

A star is a giant ball of gases—mainly hydrogen and helium. At the star's core, a process called nuclear fusion produces heat and light.

All stars form from thick clouds of gas and dust.

1. Gravity pulls the gas and dust together, which creates heat.

2. The center gets so hot that hydrogen nuclei begin to fuse together (nuclear fusion).

3. Great amounts of energy are released and a star is born.

Not all stars are equally hot.

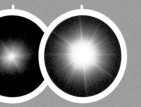

red stars (coolest)

yellow stars

white stars

blue stars (hottest)

Out of the stars in the entire universe, scientists think that:

0.0000000000005%
ARE IN OUR GALAXY, THE MILKY WAY

99.9999999999995%
ARE IN OTHER GALAXIES

70 sextillion
(70,000 million million million or 70,000,000,000,000,000,000,000)

THE AUSTRALIAN NATIONAL UNIVERSITY'S CALCULATION OF HOW MANY STARS THERE ARE IN THE UNIVERSE

No one is certain how many stars there are, though; stars are dying and being born all the time. The National Aeronautics and Space Administration (NASA) says there are "zillions," an uncountable number.

How stars die

Medium-sized stars die when they run out of hydrogen.

They grow huge, turning into a red giant that can be millions of kilometers across.

After that, they shrink down and become a white dwarf.

red giant star

white dwarf star

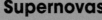

One teaspoon of matter from a white dwarf would weigh as much as three elephants (about 15 tonnes).

Supernovas

Some giant stars explode into supernovas. These may eventually become black holes (see page 16).

supernova

Black holes

Black holes are among the strangest objects in the universe. They are not actually holes, but they are completely black.

A black hole is a spot in space where gravity is so strong that nothing can escape. Even light cannot leave a black hole, which is why we cannot see them.

Formation

Black holes usually form when a large star collapses. As this happens, a huge amount of matter is squashed into a tiny area.

Because it contains so much matter, the black hole has very strong gravity.

Black holes come in different sizes, depending on how much matter they contain.

The smallest black holes are the size of an atom, but contain as much matter as Mount Everest.

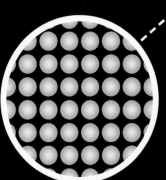

"Supermassive" black holes have as much matter as a million or more suns.

Bigger, "stellar" black holes could contain as much matter as 20 suns.

100%
OF KNOWN LARGE GALAXIES HAVE A SUPERMASSIVE BLACK HOLE AT THEIR CENTER

4,000,000
THE NUMBER OF SUNS IT WOULD TAKE TO EQUAL THE AMOUNT OF MATTER IN THE BLACK HOLE SAGITTARIUS A

Sagittarius A is the supermassive black hole at the center of our Milky Way galaxy (pictured).

Finding black holes

Scientists can locate black holes by looking at nearby stars and gases. The black hole's strong gravity affects how these behave. Stars orbiting closest to the black hole move faster because the force of gravity on them is stronger.

Galaxies

A galaxy is a huge area filled with dust, gas, and billions of stars. The gravity of a supermassive black hole helps hold each one together.

Forming star systems

The earliest galaxies discovered so far formed about one billion years after the Big Bang. Groups of stars gathered to form small galaxies.

Small, early galaxies often crashed together and formed larger ones.

Our own galaxy, the Milky Way, formed in this way.

1,892,146,094,516,160,000 km

APPROXIMATE DIAMETER OF THE MILKY WAY.

Earth is 12,755 km in diameter.

clusters of galaxies (the bright dots) in deep space

How many galaxies are there?

We used to think there were about 200 billion galaxies in the universe.

Then, in 2016, NASA estimated that there might be as many as 2 trillion (or 2,000,000,000,000).

10%

OF THE UNIVERSE'S GALAXIES CAN BE SEEN BY SCIENTISTS

90%
OF GALAXIES CANNOT BE SEEN WITH TODAY'S TELESCOPES

Galactic gravity

Galaxies contain a huge amount of matter—not only the supermassive black hole at their center, but also stars, planets and other matter.

Because galaxies contain so much matter, they have strong gravity.

Hungry galaxies

Larger galaxies sometimes "eat" smaller ones.

This happens when the gravity of the larger galaxy pulls in and slowly absorbs the smaller one.

The Andromeda galaxy is approaching our own, smaller Milky Way at approximately 10 km per second. That's 36,000 kph!

Fortunately, Andromeda is a LONG way away.

It will only eat the Milky Way in 3.75 billion years or more. Few stars will actually collide, but future life forms will see a billion-year-long light show in the night sky as stars shift position.

The solar system

A solar system is a group of planets, all held in position by a star's gravity. The star holding our solar system together is the sun.

Super-sized

The solar system is enormous. The Voyager 1 spacecraft was launched in 1977. In 2012, it reached the edge of the solar system, 18 billion km away. At this point, its radio signal took 16 hours to reach Earth.

Mercury   Venus   Earth   Mars

The sun is by far the biggest object in the solar system.

99.8%
OF THE SOLAR SYSTEM'S MASS IS CONTAINED IN THE SUN

0.2%
IS CONTAINED IN PLANETS, MOONS, AND THE REST OF SPACE

There are eight planets (large objects with a clear orbit) in the solar system.

Dwarf planet

Pluto

Pluto used to be called a planet. In 2006, however, it was downgraded to "dwarf planet" status, as it is actually part of a neighborhood of icy bodies called the Kuiper Belt objects.

Asteroids

Asteroids are rocky worlds without any atmosphere, too small to be called planets. There are tens of thousands of them between Mars and Jupiter; this region is called the asteroid belt.

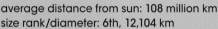

asteroids in space

Jupiter

Saturn

Uranus

Neptune

Mercury
average distance from sun: 57 million km
size rank/diameter: 8th, 4,880 km

Venus
average distance from sun: 108 million km
size rank/diameter: 6th, 12,104 km

Earth
average distance from sun: 150 million km
size rank/diameter: 5th, 12,756 km

Mars
average distance from sun: 228 million km
size rank/diameter: 7th, 6,787 km

Jupiter
average distance from sun: 778 million km
size rank/diameter: 1st, 142,800 km

Saturn
average distance from sun: 1,427 million km
size rank/diameter: 2nd, 120,536 km

Uranus
average distance from sun: 2,870 million km
size rank/diameter: 3rd, 50,724 km

Neptune
average distance from sun: 4,497 million km
size rank/diameter: 4th, 49,244 km

The sun

The sun is a 1,400,000 km-wide ball of super-hot gas at the center of the solar system. It is mostly made up of hydrogen and helium, but it contains small amounts of other gases too.

41%
OF THE SUN'S LIFE HAS PASSED

Middle-aged

The sun was born 4.5 billion years ago. Scientists think it has enough hydrogen left to burn for another 6.5 billion years.

52%
IS STILL TO COME

1,300,000
THE NUMBER OF EARTHS THAT COULD FIT INSIDE THE SUN BY VOLUME

The sun has a mass of 2 nonillion kg (2 followed by 30 zeros), or 330,000 Earths. This gives it very strong gravity.

Earth

sun

The sun: a massive ball of burning gas

hydrogen atoms fusing together

heat and light

Solar reactor

A chemical reaction is always happening in the sun's fiery core:

- The sun's powerful gravity crushes hydrogen atoms, which fuse together.
- Energy in the form of heat and light is released.
- Heat and light radiate out into space.

Plants use the energy of the sun to grow.

Sun and Earth

Even from 150,000,000 km away, the sun's heat and light still reach us. Once they arrive, the sun's heat and light:

- drive our weather, creating winds and clouds
- make the planet warm enough for life to survive

Death of the sun

When the sun runs out of hydrogen, it will die in three stages:

1. Red giant: the core shrinks and the outer layers grow massive.

2. White dwarf: the outer layers drift off into space, leaving behind a small, cooling core.

3. Black dwarf: the core loses all its heat and becomes dark.

23

Earth

Earth is a planet traveling around the sun. It is held in position by the sun's gravity.

As Earth travels around the sun, the sun's gravity pulls it closer. At the same time, Earth is trying to move away from the sun in a straight line, called sideways motion. This creates Earth's orbit.

Earth's direction of travel

Earth

orbit

sun

sun's gravity pulling Earth

As it orbits the sun, Earth also rotates on an axis. These rotations create the cycle of day and night.

our planet from space

5,000,000 km
VARIATION IN EARTH'S DISTANCE FROM THE SUN

Earth's orbit around the sun is not perfectly round. Instead, it is elliptical, or oval-shaped. This means that Earth's distance from the sun varies between 147 million km and 152 million km.

Like Earth, all the other planets in the solar system have elliptical orbits.

circular

elliptical

Earth's atmosphere

Earth's gravity holds gases close to its surface and stops them from drifting into space. Earth also has a magnetic field that surrounds the planet and stops the sun's radiation from blowing the gases away.

It is this mix of gases surrounding our planet that makes life on Earth possible. Mars used to have an atmosphere, but without a magnetic field, it was all blown away by solar radiation.

EARTH'S ATMOSPHERE IS

78%

NITROGEN

21%

OXYGEN

1%

CARBON DIOXIDE AND OTHER GASES (ARGON, NEON, HELIUM, KRYPTON AND HYDROGEN)

Nitrogen

The nitrogen in the atmosphere has no color or smell and does not usually react with other chemicals.

Oxygen

Without oxygen, animals, including humans, cannot survive. We breathe it in and use it to provide our bodies with energy.

Carbon dioxide

Carbon dioxide keeps plants alive. They use the carbon for growth and energy, and they release oxygen.

Hours and days

We measure time using units based on Earth's rotation and orbit around the sun.

Egyptian hours

The idea of hours comes from the ancient Egyptians.

They divided the day and the night into 12 units each. This created 24 units of time between sunrises.

There were 24 units of time in an Egyptian day and night, but these units could be different lengths. For example, a daytime unit would be longer in the summer, when there was more daylight.

Hours are named after the ancient Egyptian god Horus (above).

Clocks and time dictate much of our daily lives.

Modern days

Times have changed since the days of the ancient Egyptians.

Modern days are divided into 24 equal-length hours. Each day starts at 00:00 and ends at 23:59.59. Each hour lasts 60 minutes. The ancient Egyptians did not count minutes.

Most people think 24 hours is the time it takes the Earth to spin once on its axis—but this is not 100% correct.

noon

east

west

path of the sun across the sky in a day

sunrise

sunset

horizon

99.37%
OF EACH 24 HOURS COMES FROM THE EARTH'S ROTATION

0.23%
COMES FROM EARTH'S ORBIT AROUND THE SUN

3 minutes, 18 seconds

AMOUNT OF TIME ADDED TO THE PERIOD BETWEEN SUNRISES BY EARTH'S MOVEMENT AROUND THE SUN

Earth spins completely around in 23:56.42. The extra 3:18 makes 24 hours in total.

Longer days

The Earth spins more slowly as time goes on, making days longer.

Back when dinosaurs walked the Earth 100 million years ago, there were 23 hours between sunrises. In 140 million years' time, it is expected to be 25 hours.

The length of each Earth day is slowing down due to the effects of the moon's gravitational pull. Earth days are lengthening by 1.7 milliseconds each century.

1 second
AMOUNT OF TIME ADDED EVERY FEW YEARS TO ADJUST TIME BECAUSE OF EARTH'S SLOWER SPIN

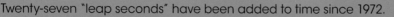
Twenty-seven "leap seconds" have been added to time since 1972.

Standardizing time

Around the world, days start and finish at different times. The sun comes up a little later as you travel further west. Wherever you are, the sun always rises in the east because of the direction the Earth spins.

town clock, Bolton, UK

In the past, towns used to have their own time.

The town clock was set to 12:00 at the moment the sun reached its highest point. Everyone else in that town set their own watches and clocks by it.

**Newfoundland
-3½ hours**

**Venezuela
-4½ hours**

Trouble with trains

In the 1800s, having different times in different towns began to cause trouble. Trains would leave the station at 12:00 and travel west for exactly six hours, but arrive BEFORE 6:00.

Something had to be done.

-11 -10 -9 -8 -7 -6 -5 -4 -3 -2

Standard time

The British decided to set their clocks according to when the sun was highest above the Royal Observatory at Greenwich, London. They called this Greenwich Mean Time, or GMT.

In 1884, the world decided to use GMT as its Coordinated Universal Time, or UTC.

Greenwich, UK

Time zones

Even though there is one standard time, it is not the same time everywhere.

Today, time zones exist to account for the differences between sunrise times in different parts of the world.

The time zones are a set number of hours behind or ahead of UTC.

London +0 hours

Iran +3½ hours

Afghanistan +3½ hours

Nepal +5¾ hours

India +5½ hours

Northern Territory +9½ hours

South Australia +9½–10½ hours

100%

OF THE WORLD BASES ITS TIME ON COORDINATED UNIVERSAL TIME

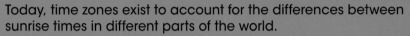

| 0 | +1 | +2 | +3 | +4 | +5 | +6 | +7 | +8 | +9 | +10 | +11 | +12 | -12 | -11 |

Glossary

asteroid belt
The area of space between the planets Mars and Jupiter where there are many asteroids, or rocky bodies too small to be planets.

astronomer
A person who studies space, the stars, planets and other bodies that make it up.

atom
A tiny particle with a core of neutrons and protons, which is surrounded by electrons. An atom is the smallest unit of matter that still has the properties, or qualities, of that matter.

celestial
An object in space with enough mass to be important in some way.

core
The center of an object.

electron
A subatomic (smaller than an atom) particle with a negative electrical charge.

element
A chemical that cannot be broken down into something else, made of only one type of atom.

elliptical
Something that is oval or egg-shaped.

galaxy
A group of billions or trillions of stars, held together by gravity.

gravity
The force of attraction, or pulling, that depends on an object's mass. Larger objects, such as stars and planets, have greater gravity than smaller objects, like those on Earth.

mass
Matter; a planet's mass, for example, is the amount of matter it contains.

matter
A physical substance that has three main forms: solid, liquid, and gas.

mean
The average, worked out by adding up several amounts, then dividing them by their number. For example, the mean of 6, 8, 10 and 13 is $(6 + 8 + 10 + 13) \div 4 = 9.25$.

neutron
A tiny particle (smaller than an atom) with no electrical charge.

nuclear fusion
The process where the cores, or nuclei, of two atoms fuse together, releasing great amounts of energy.

orbit
The circular or (more often) elliptical path taken by one object around another one.

particle
A very small piece of matter.

proton
A subatomic with a positive electrical charge.

radiation
Energy traveling through space. Sunlight is the form of radiation we feel most often.

FURTHER INFORMATION

Books to read

How Things Work In Outer Space
Paul Mason (Wayland 2018)
Part of the *Cause, Effect and Chaos!* series, this book explores space phenomena such as meteorites, black holes, and astronauts turning pee into water—as well as what happens when these things go wrong!

Record-Breaking Earth and Space Facts
Jon Richards and Ed Simkins (Hungry Tomato, 2015)
Part of the *Top Tens* series, this book features record-breaking facts such as the solar system's tallest mountain, the planet hot enough to melt metal, and more.

The Sun Is Kind Of A Big Deal
Nick Seluk (Scholastic, 2018)
This book is a fun way to explore the sun's role at the center of the solar system, with comic-style art, bite-sized chunks of text, and lots of snippets of interesting information.

Places to visit

American Space Museum & Walk of Fame
308 Pine Street
Titusville, FL 32796

This museum features artifacts donated by astronauts and NASA workers, real launch consoles, and free monthly astronomy events. Visit spacewalkoffame.org to learn more.

National Air and Space Museum
6th Street and Independence Avenue SW
Washington, DC 20560

The Smithsonian's National Air and Space Museum includes exhibitions and artifacts that showcase the history of flight, from the first airplane to modern-day space travel. More information is available at airandspace.si.edu.

Virginia Air & Space Science Center
600 Settlers Landing Road
Hampton, VA 23669

Visitors to this museum, which is the official visitor center for NASA Langley Research Center, will learn about the science of space exploration through interactive exhibits. Learn more at vasc.org.

HOW TO READ BIG NUMBERS

1,000,000,000,000,000,000,000,000,000,000 = one nonillion
1,000,000,000,000,000,000,000,000,000 = one octillion
1,000,000,000,000,000,000,000,000 = one septillion
1,000,000,000,000,000,000,000 = one sextillion
1,000,000,000,000,000,000 = one quintillion
1,000,000,000,000,000 = one quadrillion
1,000,000,000,000 = one trillion
1,000,000,000 = one billion
1,000,000 = one million
1,000 = one thousand
100 = one hundred
10 = ten
1 = one

Index

Alpha Centauri 11
Andromeda 19
antimatter 10, 12
asteroids 4, 21
astronomers 8
atmosphere 21, 25
atoms 6, 11–12, 23
Australian National
  University, the 15

Big Bang 5–7, 12,
  18
black holes 13, 15–17

cosmic rays 9

dark matter 12–13

electrons 10–11
European Space
  Agency 11

galaxies 4, 7, 10–11,
  17–19
Galilei, Galileo 8
gamma rays 9
gravity 5, 16–17, 19–20,
  22–24
Greenwich Mean
  Time (GMT) 29

helium 11, 14, 22,
  25
Horus 26
Hubble, Edwin 10

hydrogen 22–23, 25,
  11, 14–15

International Space
  Station, the (ISS) 9

James Webb Space
  Telescope 19

Kuiper Belt objects 21

Lemaître, George 6
light years 11

Massive Compact
  Halo Objects
  (MACHOS) 13
matter 6, 10, 12–13,
  16–17, 19
Milky Way, the 15,
  17–19

NASA 15, 18
neutrons 10
nuclear fusion 14
nuclei 10–11, 14

orbit 9–10, 17, 24,
  26–27

particles 5–6, 9–10
planets 4–5, 20–21, 24
Pluto 21
protons 10
Proxima Centauri 4

radiation 9, 12
red giant 15, 23

Sagittarius A 17
satellites 9
sound 9
space junk 9
spacecraft 9, 20
stars 4–6, 9, 11, 14–15,
  18–19
supernova 15

telescopes 8, 10, 19
time zones 29

Voyager 1 20

Weakly Interacting
  Massive Particles
  (WIMPS) 13
weather 23
white dwarf 15, 23

X-rays 9